The Little Book of Street Rods

by Jule-Ann Lattimer

Richard C. Owen Publishers, Inc.
Katonah, New York

My dad took me
to a street rod show.

Street rods are old cars
that are all fixed up with new parts
and shiny paint.

Some street rods at the show had big motors.

Some had big fenders.

Some had no fenders.

Some pulled little trailers.

I saw a street rod truck, too.

The coolest street rods
had flames painted on them.

Some street rods were
just my size.

The one I liked best
was my dad's street rod.